A JOL

Other titles in this series:
Let Your Artist Out!
God's Space in You
Discover Your Spirituality
Give Yourself a Break
What do You Want from Life?
What is Your God like?
Christian Meditation – Your Daily Practice
Finding The Right Retreat for You

FINDING YOUR CENTRE
A JOURNEY WITH THOMAS MERTON

JIM FOREST

Series editor Jeanne Hinton

Copyright © 1994 Hunt & Thorpe
Text © Jim Forest
Cover Illustration © Len Munnik

ISBN 1 85608 103 6

In Australia this book is published by:
Hunt & Thorpe Australia Pty Ltd.
9 Euston Street, Rydalmere NSW 2116

A CIP catalogue record for this book is available from the British Library

Manufactured in the United Kingdom

'WITHOUT KNOWING ANYTHING ABOUT IT, I BECAME A PILGRIM...'

SETTING off to see what's over the horizon is a tendency that goes back to Adam and Eve. Today it's usually called tourism. In Chaucer's day, you weren't a tourist but a pilgrim. It wasn't a summer tan you were seeking but a miracle, not necessarily the marvel of a sick person becoming suddenly well or a blind person recovering his sight. It could be the kind of miracle invisible to anyone but the one to whom it happened – the miracle of forgiveness, of overcoming a destructive obsession, or coming to a deep sense of the reality of God.

■ FROM TOURIST TO PILGRIM

It was a hidden miracle that happened to Thomas Merton during a visit to Rome in the spring of 1933 before entering Clare College in Cambridge.

Merton – 17 years old and already an orphan – was staying in a *pensione* on the Piazza Barberini. For days he had been walking Rome's tourist track, guidebook in hand. Many of the usual sights left him yawning. The architecture, statuary and painting of the Empire, the Renaissance and the Counter-Reformation struck him as vapid and melodramatic.

But Rome's more ancient churches – San Clemente, Santa Sabina, Santa Maria Maggiore, Saints Cosmas and Damian, the Lateran, Santa Costanza – moved him in an unexpected and extraordinary way. These were all churches of sober design whose main decoration were mosaic icons, images of simplicity and quiet intensity that have little in common with the theatrical art that was eventually to take over in Rome.

'I was fascinated by these Byzantine mosaics,' he wrote years later. 'I began to haunt the churches where they were to be found.'

It was as if the icons were windows to heaven. Through them he felt Christ's gaze. 'For the first time in my whole life I began to find out something of who this Person was that men call Christ... It is the Christ of the Apocalypse, the Christ the Martyrs, the Christ of the Fathers. It is the Christ of Saint John, and of Saint Paul... It is Christ God, Christ King.'

Eager to understand the images that so arrested his eyes, Merton bought a Bible. ' read more and more of the Gospels, and my love for the old churches and their mosaics grew from day to day.' Their attraction wasn't simply his appreciation of the aesthetics of iconography but the profound sense of peace he experienced within such walls. He had a deep and strong conviction that he belonged there.

He desperately wanted to pray, to light a candle and to kneel down, to pray with his body as well as his mind, but found the prospect of publicly kneeling in a church alarming.

Yet one morning, in the fifth century Church of Santa Sabina on the Aventine Hill above the Tiber, he found it impossible to play the guidebook-studying tourist any longer.

'...although the church was almost empty, I

walked across the stone floor mortally afraid that a poor devout old Italian woman was following me with suspicious eyes.'

He knelt down at the altar rail and again and again recited the Lord's Prayer.

Leaving the church, he felt a depth of joy he hadn't known in years. 'Without knowing anything about it, I became a pilgrim.'

In the years that followed Merton would find his way to Christianity, join the Catholic Church, enter a Trappist monastery, and write an autobiography *(The Seven Storey Mountain)* and many other books being read today in every part of the world.

■ EXERCISES:

Think about key elements in the story of Merton in Rome: going on pilgrimage; being alone; being silent; reading the New Testament; praying with icons; and praying both in mind and in body. For countless people, these are all normal elements in their spiritual life.

Plan a walk that will bring you past one or more churches. Make it a point to stop in at least one of them. Look around in a quiet and unhurried way. Be open to anything in the building's art or architecture that might make it easier to move from the role of observer to a person who prays.

■ OVERCOMING EMBARRASSMENT

Harder than praying that day in Santa Sabina's was Merton's act of crossing the stone floor, the sound of each step echoing throughout the building, and finally getting down on his knees, and entering into a silence far louder than his footsteps. It was acutely embarrassing for Merton, a student with a sophisticated, intellectual background.

It wasn't only the old Italian woman whom he imagined was watching him with suspicion (probably she saw at a glance the struggle the young man was going through and was busy praying for him). Merton's most critical audience was himself: Merton watching Merton. Even had the church been empty, he would have been embarrassed.

'What can we gain by sailing to the moon,' Merton asked later in life, 'if we are not able to cross the abyss that separates us from ourselves?' But how hard it is to overcome those things which separate us from ourselves.

Probably far more people today would be embarrassed being seen at prayer than was the case in 1933. The sort of chagrin that once would have been experienced by the person with a erotic magazine or novel in hand is today more likely to be felt by the person with a Bible in the open. The number of people going to church in most countries falls a bit more each year. It's no longer surprising to hear a phrase of Merton's – the post-Christian era – applied to the time we live in.

Whether among friend or strangers, the pressure to conform to certain behavioural patterns has tidal strength. We know what is expected of us. We know we are living in a secular society which half suspects the religious believer of being mentally unbalanced.

It's helpful to be aware of what we're up against, of what it means to live in a secular society in which it is easier to be good consumers than devout people.

The theologian Alexander Schmemann, whose books came to be much admired by Merton, defined secularism as 'above all *a negation of worship*... the negation of man as a worshiping being.' ('Worship in a Secular World' in *For the Life of the World*) Far from being the most central human action, worship in such a society is relegated to the category of hobby or diversion.

Approaching the communion rail in Santa Sabina's, Merton was taking his first awkward steps away from the unwritten laws imposed by secular society.

■ EXERCISES:

Merton had to overcome embarrassment in order to begin his spiritual journey. Are there actions you would tend to avoid either because they mark you too publicly as being religious or because you come from a religious background that tends to avoid external actions?

Do you see embarrassment as an obstacle to going further in developing your spiritual life? If so, can you think of any action, however small, that you might take that would help you go further?

Become more aware of the ways in which you

conform to the expectations of others employers, teachers, parents and friends, even strangers.

Get a pocket-sized New Testament and use it as often as you can. Do you find yourself reluctant to read it on the bus or underground? What is it that makes it easier to read a newspaper in public than a Bible?

■ LINKING THE SPIRITUAL AND THE PHYSICAL

'There is always the chance to step over the line and enter into simple and contemplative union with God,' Merton wrote in *The Sign of Jonas*.

Crossing that border often requires linking the physical and the spiritual.

It was a momentous event in Merton's life when he made his way to the communion rail in Santa Sabina's and got down on his knees: a physical as well as spiritual action. If he had simply stood somewhere in the church, it wouldn't have been the same thing.

Finding a physical response that is appropriate to a spiritual action is at the heart of religious life. This isn't surprising. After all, Christianity is an incarnational religion. Jesus washed the dirt from his feet, held people in his arms, slept at night, knew hunger and thirst, and cried tears just as wet as any of us ever shed. The blood in his veins was like the blood in our veins. He was God, but God *incarnate*. Like us, he was flesh and blood.

Even its view of heaven stresses the physical. It wasn't the ghost of Jesus that presented itself to the disciples after the crucifixion. We see Thomas understanding what he had heard and witnessed only after he had placed his hand in one of the wounds in Christ's body. We are told about the resurrected Jesus eating baked fish with his disciples. We too will be raised body and soul from death, an event prefigured in Christ's resurrection.

While the spiritual life of its nature must be lived body and soul, it is one of the misfortunes of history that many forms of Christianity have gradually become more spiritualised, in the sense of minimising the physical.

It was once the case that Christians everywhere often made the sign of the cross on their bodies, reciting with this gesture the words, 'In the name of the Father, the Son and the Holy Spirit.' This action was a re-connection with God, a way of saying *amen* in both body and soul.

It used to be in all Christian churches, and still

is in Orthodox churches, a custom to kiss icons and the Bible. There was the lighting of candles, a simple analogy for the light that is always struck by prayer, an action that is in itself so inviting that it inspires prayer. It was once normal for Christians either to stand or kneel while praying, both physical postures which experience has shown help dispose us to prayer.

Similarly any relationship of love has both its physical and spiritual dimensions. Ideally the two become indistinguishably joined in ways appropriate to the relationship. A husband and wife not only verbally express their love to each other but make love with their bodies, fulfilling the marriage vow, 'With my body I thee worship.' A child not only needs spoken assurance of love from a parent but needs to be held, needs to be kissed good night, and needs a parent's hands at moments of anxiety.

Eating together is a ritual of friendship that has immense spiritual significance. A meal cooked with love is different than a meal that is simply served up. It was at a table among his disciples that Christ took bread and wine and linked them forever with his body and blood.

Developing the spiritual life is often simply recognising the possibilities for prayer hidden within ordinary things we are already doing. In any physical action that isn't of its nature at odds with the spiritual life, there is the possibility of prayer, from washing dishes to building a house.

The big step is often just imagining the possibilities of spiritual life that exist in the most ordinary activities, then trying to find ways so that the two reinforce each other.

■ EXERCISES:

Experiment with the connection between body posture and prayer. Keep in mind that in the early days of Christianity, chairs and pews were not part of church design and that in general people stood unless infirmity or tiredness required sitting. Try some standing prayer.

While involved in routine actions like washing the dishes, try reciting the Jesus Prayer: 'Lord Jesus Christ, Son of God, have mercy on me a sinner.'

It used to be common for all Christians to make the sign of the cross many times every day. Unless you are Catholic, Anglo-Catholic or Orthodox, you may feel you have no right to such a custom yet feel a certain envy for those whose tradition encourages such gestures. If only privately, try making the sign of the cross on your body whenever you say, 'In the name of the Father, the Son and the Holy Spirit.' There may come a time when you feel at home in doing this even in situations in which you are the only one doing so, or at table before beginning a meal.

Think about how you feel as you experiment with drawing together physical and spiritual actions. You may experience a complex mixture of excitement and anxiety, much as a student feels in the early days of speaking an acquired language with a native speaker.

■ LOOKING FOR THIN PLACES

'As soon as you get in your groove, boy do things happen,' Merton wrote to a friend some years after discovering his monastic vocation.

During Holy Week in 1941, Merton travelled from the college in upstate New York where he was teaching English literature, to the Trappist monastery of Our Lady of Gethsemani in rural Kentucky.

Unpacking his suitcase in the monastery guest house, Merton was overwhelmed with the sense that he had finally found the centre he was looking for. 'I should tear out all the pages of this book,' he wrote in his journal, 'and all the other pages of anything else I have ever written, and begin here. This is the centre of America. I had wondered what was holding the country together, what has been keeping the universe from cracking in pieces and falling apart. It is places like this monastery – not only this one: there must be others.'

Changes in recent years have softened many of the sharp edges in Trappist life as Merton found it. A monk of Gethsemani today has his own small room, freedom to correspond and to follow world news, and warmth in the winter. In 1941 monastic life was more austere. The monks slept in their robes on straw-covered boards in dormitories that were frigid in winter and sweltering in summer. Beds were separated by shoulder-high partitions. Half the year was fasting time. A typical meal featured bread, potatoes, an apple, and barley coffee. In those days the fire wasn't lit until frost had iced the church windows. Hot water was on tap two days a week. A novice's few personal possessions were kept in a small box in the scriptorium. Hard manual labour was done with tools that had changed little since medieval times. News from the outside world rarely reached the monks. Communication was mainly by sign language. Barring special permission, mail to the outside world could be sent only four times a year: Easter, Assumption, All Saints, and Christmas, and then only four half-page letters. Delivery of mail was normally restricted to the same four feasts.

Strange as it may seem, Merton felt at home in that harsh environment in a way he had never felt before. On December 10, he returned, this time to be received as a novice. He moved from the world of noise and careers to a community of silence and worship.

While every search has its hidden, inner reality, actively searching for places that help make us more aware of God, more vulnerable to God, is a normal element of spiritual life.

It's worth thinking about travel not just as a time to get away but as a time to search, and to aim for places which have a reputation for being 'thin places' – places where you can sense God's presence in much the way you smell warm bread in an oven. It doesn't have to be far away, but it must be a place where, at the very least, you aren't embarrassed to be praying – ideally a place where you would feel odd not to pray.

■ EXERCISES:

Consider making a retreat at a monastery. An important element of monastic life is to welcome guests seeking an environment in which prayer is the main event. Let each guest be received as Jesus Christ, Saint Benedict counselled in his Holy Rule. While very few monastery guests become monks, even fewer find that a monastic environment doesn't help them see their lives and future direction more clearly, or see a way through a problem which had previously seemed hopeless. In the west, most monasteries are Catholic, in the east most are Orthodox, but you needn't belong to the church the monks are part of in order to be their guest. (A local pastor would be able to give you addresses for any number of monasteries, some of which are probably near by.)

■ HOLY SILENCE

'There is in all visible things an invisible fecundity, a dimmed light, a meek namelessness, a hidden wholeness. This mysterious Unity and Integrity is Wisdom, the Mother of all,' Merton wrote in *Hagia Sophia* (Holy Wisdom). 'There is in all things an inexhaustible sweetness and purity, a silence that is a fountain of action and of joy. It rises up in wordless gentleness and flows out to me from the unseen roots of all created being.'

The monastic order that Merton joined, the Trappists, has a profound devotion to Mary, the mother of Jesus, and also a tradition of silence.

There is an intimate connection between Mary and silence. While Mary is one of the main figures in the Gospels, she is usually silent. We hear her words only on a few occasions. What she has to say is summed up in the response she made to the Archangel Gabriel at the Annunciation – 'May it be done to me according to your word' – and in her instructions to the waiters at the marriage feast in Cana: 'Do whatever he tells you.'

We see her also struggling to understand her son's action when he was twelve and had gone to the Temple in Jerusalem without telling anyone in his family. ' His mother,' Luke comments, 'kept all these things in her heart' – that is, she thought about the mystery of her son and his actions in deep and loving silence. Mary is the archetype of the praying and listening person.

Merton writes about her silence during the period that the Christ child was within her womb:

'...far beneath the movement of this silent cataclysm Mary slept in the infinite tranquility of God, and God was a child curled up who slept in her and her veins were flooded with His wisdom which is night, which is starlight, which is silence. And her whole being was embraced in Him whom she embraced and they became tremendous silence.' (*The Ascent to Truth*, p 317)

But in this age, few of us are used to silence. I had an acquaintance in New York City who lost his job as announcer on a popular radio station when he broadcast ten seconds of silence. His employers said that for many listeners, such a prolonged silence was frightening.

Mary had the advantage of living in a culture at home with silence, a society without radios or television. No one in Nazareth was up on the 'news' in the sense we use the word today, though they knew a great deal about the world around them. Even today if you are staying in a Galilean village and go for a short walk out into the olive groves, the silence is stunning. It isn't an empty silence but the ageless talk of creation: the slight movements of the air, the sounds of birds, the abrupt motion of a lizard, the distant shouts of children playing in the village.

In 'Rain and the Rhinoceros', one sees how deeply attuned Merton became in his silence to the language of creation. The essay celebrates not only rain but everything commercial society ignores and neglects which it cannot understand, control or sell:

'Think of it: all that speech pouring down,

selling nothing, judging nobody, drenching the thick mulch of dead leaves, soaking the trees, filling the gullies and crannies of the wood with water, washing out the places where men have stripped the hillside!...this wonderful, unintelligible, perfectly innocent speech, the most comforting speech in the world, the talk that rain makes.' (*Raids on the Unspeakable*, pp 9–23)

One of the hardest struggles in developing a deeper spiritual life is to cultivate a taste for quietness – external when it can be found, and in any event to cultivate inner silence. Merton described the value of the movement toward silence in a letter written in 1967:

'The contemplative life has nothing to tell you except to reassure you and say that if you dare to penetrate your own silence and dare to advance without fear into the solitude of your own heart, and risk the sharing of that solitude with the lonely other who seeks God through you and with you, then you will truly recover the light and capacity to understand what is beyond words and beyond explanations because it is too close to be explained: it is the intimate union in the depths of your own heart, of God's spirit and your own secret inmost self, so that you and He are in truth One Spirit.' ('A Letter on the Contemplative Life,' *The Monastic Journey*, pp 169–173)

Saint Ignatius, Bishop of Antioch, a disciple of Saint John the Evangelist, made the comment: 'He who possesses in truth the word of Jesus can hear even its silence.'

■ EXERCISES:

Turn off the radio, television, and any other sources of background noise that it is in your power to disconnect. Practice listening to silence. It turns out not to be so silent.

In conversation, don't just wait your turn to speak while listening in a distracted way to another person, but listen with all the care you are capable of. Let listening become an act of prayer.

■ REPETITIVE PRAYER

'There is something in my nature that makes me dream of being a tramp,' Merton noted in his journal after seven years quite stationary years in the monastery.

If Merton never became a tramp, he did a great deal of tramping about on the extensive grounds of his monastery, much of which was heavily wooded land. His walks were an important element in his spiritual life.

The wonderful thing about walking is that it lends itself so readily to prayer. Perhaps it has to do with the slowness. Whatever may be hurrying by, it isn't you. You are in slow motion. Every step you take can be linked to a prayer.

One of the prayers that became very important to Merton in his later life was the Jesus Prayer. This is based on the words, 'Lord, have mercy,' at the heart of the story Jesus told about the contrite tax collector (Luke 18:9-14). The publican's three word appeal developed into the Jesus Prayer: 'Lord Jesus Christ, Son of God, have mercy on me a sinner.' In the Orthodox

Church, it is a prayer used not only by monks but countless others who aspire to pray without ceasing. Hundreds of thousands of people are praying it as you read these words. I find going for a walk while praying the Jesus Prayer is a particularly good way to start the day.

Keep in mind that it will take long use of the Jesus Prayer for it to do its work in your life. Think of what you are doing as analogous to planting an acorn and watering the ground in which it is hidden. It will be years before it is a deeply rooted tree.

One of the items with Merton on his trip to Asia was a rosary. You don't see them very often these days. It might take some looking around to find one, but it's worth the search. This touching of knots (or spheres of wood, stone or metal) with your finger tips can help further connect the action of the body with the action of the soul and make it easier to remain undistracted.

There is no end of short texts that can be recited while walking. Thousands of verses in the Bible lend themselves to such use, and there are many other prayers that, once memorised, prove useful under particular circumstances and which seem to recite themselves when needed.

But what's the point of repeating a few words over and over again?

The mind can be a cluttered place, every bit as noisy as the loudest radio station. Worries, strategies, ambitions, chores, irritations – all these easily take over to the point we hardly know where we are. We see and hear what's something of happening around us, but mechanically. We are able to move from place to place and make more or less appropriate responses to those around us, but the contact is often so superficial that it borders on being deaf and blind. In such a state, God is at best an idea, not an encounter.

Repetitive prayer helps create an inner quiet and clear away the rubbish. One recovers a sense of wholeness, of being centred. One becomes more aware of God less as an idea and more as a actual presence.

Late in his life, in a talk given to his fellow

monks just before moving into a hermitage the community gave him in response to his longing for a deeper solitude, Merton said:

'Life is this simple: We are living in a world that is absolutely transparent and God is shining through it all the time. This is not just a fable or a nice story. It is true. If we abandon ourselves to God and forget ourselves, we see it sometimes, and we see it maybe frequently. God manifests Himself everywhere, in everything – in people and in things and in nature and in events. It becomes very obvious that He is everywhere and in everything and we cannot be without Him. You cannot be without God. It's impossible. It's simply impossible. The only thing is that we don't see it. What is it that makes the world opaque? It is care.' (unpublished, from a tape recording at the monastery)

By 'care' Merton didn't mean concern for the well being of others but anxiety about oneself. Any method of prayer that helps you get beyond such God-hiding anxiety is beyond value.

■ EXERCISE:

Try using the Jesus Prayer as you walk, in a quiet and beautiful place when that is possible, or along a busy street. Pray it slowly and quietly, aware of your breath. Connect the repetition of the words with the action of exhaling, while letting the act of inhaling become a breathing in of silence.

Learn and use the Hail Mary: Hail Mary, full of grace, the Lord is with you. Blessed are you among women and blessed is the fruit of your womb, Jesus. Holy Mary, Mother of God, pray for us sinners now and at the hour of our death. Amen.

Try praying the rosary. It isn't only for Catholic or Orthodox Christians. This ancient aid to prayer has helped many millions of people and might help you. Prayers said repetitively, like the Jesus Prayer and the Hail Mary, help protect inner silence. The pastor of any Catholic or Orthodox parish can help you find a rosary - prayer rope is the Orthodox term - and can explain its use.

■ PRAYING WITH ICONS

Also with Merton on his trip to Asia was a small icon of Mary and the child Jesus that had been painted on Mount Athos in Greece. Given to him in 1965 shortly after he had received permission to live in a hermitage, Merton responded to the donor, Marco Pallis in England, with a letter full of gratitude:

'How shall I begin? I have never received such a precious and magnificent gift from anyone in my life. I have no words to express how deeply moved I was to come face to face with this sacred and beautiful presence granted to me... At first I could hardly believe it... It is a perfect act of timeless worship. I never tire of gazing at it. There is a spiritual presence and reality about it, a true spiritual 'Thaboric' light, which seems unaccountably to proceed from the Heart of the Virgin and Child as if they had One heart, and which goes out to the whole universe. It is unutterably splendid. And silent. It imposes a silence on the whole hermitage... [This] icon of the Holy Mother came as a messenger at a precise moment when a message was needed, and her presence before me has been an incalculable aid in resolving a difficult problem.'

Merton in his last years had the same spiritual vulnerabilities that marked him when he was 17 and in Rome. He hadn't been moved to pray by the Renaissance and Baroque paintings. They were too much like movie posters: loud, busy, and with a cast of thousands. What stirred him deeply were icons (from the Greek word for image) on the walls of the city's most ancient churches.

Icons are as old as Christianity. 'I have seen a great many portraits of the Savior, and of Peter and Paul, which have been preserved up to our time,' Eusebius stated in his *History of the Church*, written early in the fourth century. Whether any of the icons from the first century have survived is a matter of dispute among art historians, but what is certain is that their use is rapidly spreading among Christians in churches which long avoided religious imagery.

But aren't icons idols? Only if you worship

them. In that sense, we can make idols out of almost anything. In fact icons are an affirmation of the Incarnation and a inherent component of incarnational spirituality.

'Since the invisible One became visible by taking on flesh,' St. John of Damascus explained in the 7th century in his essay on divine images, 'you can fashion the image of him who you saw. Since He who has neither body nor form nor quantity nor quality, who goes beyond all grandeur by the excellence of his nature, He, being of divine nature, took on the condition of a slave and reduced himself to quantity and quality by clothing himself in human features. Therefore, paint on wood and present for contemplation Him who desired to become visible.'

A year before his death, in a letter to a Quaker friend who didn't understand his enthusiasm for 'the Christ of the Byzantine icons,' Merton explained that the icon 'represents a traditional experience formulated in a theology of light, the icon being a kind of sacramental medium for the illumination and awareness of the glory of Christ within us... What one "sees" in prayer before an icon is not an external representation of a historical person, but an interior presence in light, which is the glory of the transfigured Christ, the experience of which is transmitted in faith from generation to generation by those who have "seen," from the Apostles on down... So when I say that my Christ is the Christ of the icons, I mean that he is reached not through any scientific study but through direct faith and the mediation of the liturgy, art, worship, prayer, theology of light, etc., that is all bound up with the Russian and Greek tradition.' (letter to June Yungblut in *The Hidden Ground of Love*)

■ EXERCISES:

It isn't hard to find good prints of icons these days, from postcard size on up. Buy one that appeals to you, put a lighted candle in front of it and simply stand in front of the icon in silence. If you attention wanders, recite the Jesus Prayer in order to return to inner silence. Or pray as the Holy Spirit moves you, silently or out loud, in word or song.

Read one of the many good books on icons now available. A particularly good starting point is Henri Nouwen's Behold the Beauty of the Lord. For a thorough introduction to iconography, there is The Meaning of Icons by Leonid Ouspensky and Vladimir Lossky.

■ THE UNDIVIDED CHURCH

The words 'new, improved!' are printed in big bright letters on many supermarket boxes. We need to consider the possibility that what is new is not necessarily better and actually might be worse. Certainly this is true of what we need to learn if we wish to go deeper in the spiritual life. While many things have been discovered that were unknown to our ancestors, few of us know as much as the Christians of the first centuries about what it meant to be a disciple of Jesus.

Think again about the churches Merton was drawn to as a young man in Rome. They were churches built centuries before the schism that divided the Greek and Latin churches from each other. They were, in a way, churches bearing witness to the undivided church, the church that was not only Catholic but catholic – that is, universal, without borders. Despite being so ancient, there is a freshness and energy about them possessed by few modern churches.

It was a hallmark of Merton's spiritual and intellectual development that he was drawn to the theologians of the early, undivided Church, and to mystics of later times who, though living in the centuries after division, experienced a oneness in their spiritual life that cut through all the barriers imposed by history, rivalries, misunderstandings, politics and money.

'If I can unite in myself the thought and devotion of Eastern and Western Christendom, the Greek and the Latin Fathers, the Russian and the Spanish mystics, I can prepare in myself the reunion of divided Christians. From that secret and unspoken unity in myself can eventually come a visible and manifest unity of all Christians. If we want to bring together what is divided, we cannot do so by imposing one division upon the other. If we do this, the union is not Christian. It is political and doomed to further conflict. We must contain all the divided worlds in ourselves and transcend them in Christ.' (*Conjectures of a Guilty Bystander*, p 12)

It was this inner movement towards union that attracted him to forms of spiritual life that were regarded by many Christians of the sixties as old-fashioned and irrelevant. But for Merton it was clear that the river was most pure at its headwaters:

'If for some reason it were necessary for you to drink a pint of water taken out of the Mississippi River and you could choose where it was to be drawn out of the river – would you take a pint from the source of the river in Minnesota or from the estuary in New Orleans? The example is perhaps not perfect. Christian tradition and spirituality does not become polluted with development. That is not the idea at all. Nevertheless, tradition and spirituality are all the more pure and genuine in proportion as they are in contact with the original source and retain the same content.' (from 'Monastic Spirituality and the Early Fathers, from the Apostolic Fathers to Evagrius Ponticus,' an unpublished essay by Thomas Merton)

Merton's attraction to the spiritual methods of the early Church has implications for every Christian no matter from what background. Nothing should be dismissed as useless in the spiritual life simply because it is old or comes from a different branch of Christianity.

'My Catholicism,' he wrote, 'is all the world and all ages. It dates from the beginning of the world. The first man was the image of Christ and contained Christ, even as he was created, as saviour of the heart. The first woman was destined to be the ancestor of the Redeemer and the first woman was the mother of all life, in the image of the Immaculate Daughter who was full of grace, Mother of mercy, Mother of the Saved.' (from *Introductions East & West* and *Honorable Reader*)

■ EXERCISES:

Find and visit an Orthodox church and attend the Holy Liturgy. You will find people in the church happy to explain what is happening. You may find the elaborate ritual and singing hard to understand but you are experiencing the least changed form of worship that exists within Christianity. No other church today uses a model of worship that goes back so many centuries.

■ UNEXPECTED EPIPHANIES

One of the important experiences in Merton's life happened while walking in Louisville in 1958, seventeen years after becoming a monk. He was in the city on an errand, at one of the city's busiest intersections, when suddenly he saw the people around him with different eyes:

'In Louisville, at the corner of Fourth and Walnut, in the centre of the shopping district, I was suddenly overwhelmed with the realization that I loved all those people, that they were mine and I theirs, that we could not be alien to one another even though we were total strangers. It was like waking from a dream of separateness, of spurious self-isolation in a special world, the world of renunciation and supposed holiness. The whole illusion of a separate holy existence is a dream...

'This sense of liberation from an illusory difference was such a relief and such a joy to me that I almost laughed out loud... It is a glorious destiny to be a member of the human race, though it is a race dedicated to many absurdities and one which makes many terrible mistakes: yet, with all that, God Himself gloried in becoming a member of the human race. A member of the human race! To think that such a commonplace realization should suddenly seem like news that one holds the winning ticket in a cosmic sweepstake. . . .

'There is no way of telling people that they are all walking around shining like the sun... There are no strangers! . . . If only we could see each other [as we really are] all the time. There would be no more war, no more hatred, no more cruelty, no more greed... I suppose the big problem would be that we would fall down and worship each other... the gate of heaven is every-where.' [*Conjectures of A Guilty Bystander*, 140-42]

In this unexpected epiphany, Merton discovered one of the main illusions that had survived his first seventeen years of monastic life – the idea that sanctity required radical separation within 'the world of renunciation and supposed holiness.'

The experience did not suggest to him that he ought to give up his monastic vocation but it marked the start of a much deeper engagement with those outside the monastery. Merton began opening more and more lines of contact and dialogue. He associated himself with the often-imprisoned Dorothy Day and her Catholic Worker community in New York City. He wrote essays on peace, racism, and human rights for the newspaper she edited and many other publications. His guests at the monastery were often people actively involved in movements for peace and justice.

Merton's experience at 4th and Walnut highlights a common difficulty confronting many people: the idea that the spiritual life has nothing to do with the ordinary events of life and still less with the political and economic order in which we live.

'It is my belief,' Merton said, ' that we should not be too sure of having found Christ in ourselves until we have found him also in that part of humanity that is most remote from our own.'

■ EXERCISES:

Practise looking at the faces of others, even those you feel threatened by, with the awareness that this person, too, was created in the image and likeness of God, however much the choices the person has made may have made it difficult to see the likeness.

Set aside some time each day to pray for others, especially for those whose well-being you find it difficult to care about. The prayer can be a variation of the Jesus prayer: 'Lord Jesus Christ, Son of God, have mercy upon...'

As you pray, give yourself time to recall the face of the person for whom you are praying.

■ SAVED BY AN ONION

In *The Brothers Karamazov*, Dostoyevsky tells the story of a woman who died and went to hell because she had been so selfish throughout her life. But her guardian angel recalled the tight-fisted woman had once, many years before, thrown an onion at a beggar in order to chase him away. The angel pointed out to God that this might be considered, in a way, the *gift* of an onion to a beggar. Agreeing, God dispatched the angel to hell, saying that the onion could now be used to pull the woman out of hell. And it nearly happened. The woman grabbed hold of the onion and was being lifted out of a sullen crowd in hell. But some of those around her grabbed hold of her and were being pulled out of hell with her. The woman, as selfish as ever, started kicking at those who had attached themselves to her. Shouting the words, 'Just for me!', the onion broke and she fell back into hell – back into the prison of her own selfishness.

The story's simple meaning: We can't go to heaven alone. We can't turn a blind eye to beggars, refugees, the homeless, to those maimed or made insane by war – or to the structures of society that create suffering.

For Merton during the last decade of his life, nothing was clearer than we live our spiritual life not on some other planet but here on earth, in the time and place where God has put us, in company with everyone and everything around us. If your neighbour is being dragged away by Nazis, or being beaten to death by racists, or being starved by famine and threatened by war, you can't say you were too busy praying to respond.

Religious renewal, Merton said, must be 'expressed in the historical context' and requires a 'spiritual understanding of historical crises, an evaluation of them in terms of their inner significance.'

What this means in practical terms in your own life depends on your vocation and particular circumstances. But a spiritual life that attempts to exist outside history is no spiritual life at all. ' Whoever says,' "I love God," but hates his brother, is a liar,' says Saint John the Evangelist in one of the sharpest passages in the New Testament, (1 John 4:20).

An admirer of Gandhi and Martin Luther King, Merton stressed nonviolent approaches to defending life and resisting injustice. 'The Christian does not need to fight and indeed it is better that he should not fight, for insofar as he imitates his Lord and Master, he proclaims that the Messianic Kingdom has come and bears witness to the presence of the *Kyrios Pantocrator* [Greek for the Lord of Creation] in mystery, even in the midst of the conflicts and turmoil of the world.' (*Seeds of Destruction*, p 129)

While identifying himself with movements for peace and social justice, Merton didn't regard those who were active in such groups uncritically. He emphasised the importance of those who are trying to save lives not imagining that they are too busy for a spiritual life. He pointed out that social activists, if they don't take great care about their inner life, can easily become self-righteous zealots inadvertently driving many people in the opposite direction. 'We are never so likely to do violence,' he noted, 'as when we are being righteous.'

He warned of the danger that exists in families, monastic communities and groups working for social change 'where the martyr for the right some times thrives on making his persecutors terribly and visibly wrong. He can drive them in desperation to be wrong, to seek refuge in the wrong, to seek refuge in violence.'

One of the great gifts a deep spiritual life offers to the socially engaged person, he said, is confidence that God will make good use of whatever constructive efforts we are making no matter how useless they seem to us at the time. Here is what he had to say about it in a letter I received from him in 1966 when I was struggling with an overwhelming sense of futility:

'Do not depend on the hope of results. When you are doing the sort of work you have taken on, essentially an apostolic work, you may have to face the fact that your work will be apparently worthless and even achieve no result at all, if not perhaps results opposite to what you expect. As you get used to this idea, you start more and more to concentrate not on the results but on the value, the rightness, the truth of the work itself. And there too a great deal has to be gone through, as gradually you struggle less and less for an idea and more and more for specific people. The range tends to narrow down, but it gets much more real. In the end, it is the reality of personal relationships that saves everything.

'You are fed up with words, and I don't blame you. I am nauseated by them sometimes. I am also, to tell the truth, nauseated by ideals and with causes. This sounds like heresy, but I think you will understand what I mean. It is so easy to get engrossed with ideas and slogans and myths that in the end one is left holding the bag, empty, with no trace of meaning left in it. And then the temptation is to yell louder than ever in order to make the meaning be there again by magic. Going through this kind of reaction helps you to guard against this. Your system is complaining of too much verbalizing, and it is right.

'... The big results are not in your hands or mine, but they suddenly happen, and we can share in them; but there is no point in building our lives on this personal satisfaction, which may be denied us and which after all is not that important.

'... All the good that you will do will come not from you but from the fact that you have allowed yourself, in the obedience of faith, to be used by God's love. Think of this more, and gradually you will be free from the need to prove yourself, and you can be more open to the power that will work through you without your knowing it.

'The great thing after all is to live, not to pour out your life in the service of a myth: and we turn the best things into myths. If you can get free from the domination of causes and just serve Christ's truth, you will be able to do more and will be less crushed by the inevitable disappointments...

'The real hope, then, is not in something we think we can do but in God who is making something good out of it in some way we cannot see. If we can do His will, we will be helping in this process. But we will not necessarily know all about it beforehand...'

■ EXERCISES:

Find out about places where the homeless and hungry are being welcomed. Volunteer some time helping out, making it a point to pray for those you encounter.

Make a list of problems in the world that trouble or frighten you and try to think about them, one by one, in the light of the actions and words of Jesus. Ask the Holy Spirit to show you how you might make a personal response to just one of the problems on your list.

■ COMMUNION

'The worst thing that can happen to a person who is already divided up into a dozen different compartments is to seal off yet another compartment and tell him that this one is more important than all the others, and that he must henceforth exercise a special care in keeping it separate from them...

'The first thing that you have to do, before you start thinking about such a thing as contemplation, is to try to recover your basic natural unity, to reintegrate your compartmentalised being into a co-ordinated and simple whole, and learn to live as a unified human person. This means that you have to bring back together the fragments of your distracted existence so that when you say "I" there is really someone present to support the pronoun you have uttered. (*The Inner Experience*, part I, *Cistercian Studies*, 1983, p 122)

Throughout his adult life Merton sought a deeper integration within himself. He became ever more convinced that the spiritual life is that healing and awakening process which brings us into a state of communion – with God, with each other, and with creation – no matter how deep and irreconcilable the divisions that confront us may appear to be. 'We must contain all the divided worlds in ourselves,' he wrote in *Conjectures of a Guilty Bystander*, 'and transcend them in Christ.' 'The search for communion' he said, 'is something that the deepest ground of our being cries out for, and it is something for which a lifetime of striving would not be enough.' (*Asian Journal*, p 316)

To be in communion with others, to see the divine presence instead of a world of postcard-flatness, requires being in communion with both God and oneself – to have reached a state of wholeness in which the "I" is authentic: the "I" who stands in the presence of God. It is not the "I" of masks and destructive appetites created by advertising or by the demands of others who want in some way to make us useful parts in an economic or political machine.

In that sense, the spiritual life implies a

relentless battle with anything drawing us into a state of division and illusion. For this reason Merton at times described the monastic life as partly an act of protest – but his insight applies to the spiritual life no matter in what context it is it lived.

'By my monastic life and vows I am saying No to all the concentration camps, the aerial bombardments, the staged political trials, the judicial murders, the racial injustices, the economic tyrannies, and the whole socio-economic apparatus which seems geared for nothing but global destruction in spite of all its fair words in favor of peace. I make monastic silence a protest against the lies of politicians, propagandists and agitators, and when I speak it is to deny that my faith and my Church can ever seriously be aligned with these forces of injustice and destruction.' (from the preface to the Japanese edition of *The Seven Storey Mountain*; see *Introductions East & West*, or *Honorable Reader*)

Merton was a devout, orthodox, intensely Christ-centred person who recited the Creed with conviction and sought in every way to follow Christ; he received the Eucharist almost every day from the early days of his conversion until the end of his life. Yet his contemplative experience made it possible for him to experience communion with many from other religious traditions – Jews, Moslems, Buddhists and Hindus – who were regarded by many Christians as being on the other side of insurmountable walls.

Speaking to a largely non-Christian audience in Calcutta in 1968 only weeks before his death, he said, 'The deepest level of communication is...communion. It is wordless. It is beyond words, and it is beyond speech, and it is beyond concept. Not that we discover a new unity. We discover an older unity... we are already one. But we imagine that we are not. What we have to recover is our original unity. What we have to be is what we are.' (*Asian Journal*, p 308)

■ EXERCISES:

Consider Merton's view that compartmentalisation is a major problem in the spiritual lives of many people: work in one box, family another, politics in a third, and religion in yet another isolated space. How true is this in your own life? Can you imagine bringing your life into greater unity?

Note that Merton avoided theological argument but was eager to discuss with people living in other religious traditions their ways of prayer and meditation. What experience have you of discussion with those whose religious views and practices are different? Has it been discussion about teaching? Or practice?

Think about Merton's words, 'We all stand on the hidden ground of love.' Can you identify lines of connection between yourself and others whose religious tradition is quite different?

■ FOLLOWING CHRIST

We can become so engrossed is something we call spiritual life that there is the danger of it becoming an end in itself. Merton made much the same warning about the term 'contemplation':

'The word "contemplation" does not occur in the Gospel,' he pointed out. 'The idea of abstracting oneself from all things, purifying one's mind of all images, and ascending by self-denial to an ecstatic intellectual contact with God the Supreme Truth – ending up by being "alone with the alone" – all this...has been taken over by a whole tradition of Christian writers and has been christianised. But still we must...take care not to lose sight of Christ Himself and His teachings in order to follow a more or less pagan line of thought from which Christ is all but excluded.' ('Monastic Spirituality and the Early Fathers, from the Apostolic Fathers to Evagrius Ponticus')

What mattered to Merton in those ancient churches he visited in Rome at age 17 was not a form of Christian art or an ecstatic experience that he hoped he might occasionally re-experience in the future; what mattered was 'his Person...Christ... It is the Christ of the Apocalypse, the Christ of the Martyrs, the Christ of the Fathers. It is the Christ of Saint John, and of Saint Paul... It is Christ God, Christ King.

Spiritual life for a Christian is a way of describing how we pursue a Christ-centred life and discovering what we can learn from the experience of others who have set off to do the same thing. Monks especially learnt quite a lot about how to pray, how to quiet the mind, how to connect body and soul, and all these things can help us along our way no matter what our vocation, temperament, age, degrees or test scores.

But the object of our pilgrimage isn't the accumulation of spiritual techniques or a pleasant state of mind or self-esteem or positive ideas or better health or longer life or economic security but Christ: the Christ of the Apocalypse, the Christ of the Martyrs, the Christ of the Saints,

Christ God, Christ King.

Drawing from the tradition of the Russian mystics, another way of saying the same thing is to say the object of the spiritual life is to acquire the Holy Spirit. This is precisely what the word 'spirituality' is about. The most loved of Russian saints, Seraphim of Sarov, used to say, 'Acquire the Holy Spirit and thousands of souls around you will be saved.'

We experience Christ through the Holy Spirit. It is the Holy Spirit who guides and sustains us as followers of Christ. There is no Christian spirituality that isn't Christ-centred. And there is no Christian spirituality that doesn't seek to acquire the Holy Spirit.

Where this will lead, none of us knows, only that the Christ whom we seek will himself accompany us along the way. As Merton put it in a prayer:

'My Lord God, I have no idea where I am going. I do not see the road ahead of me. I cannot know for certain where it will end. Nor do I really know myself, and the fact that I think

I am following your will does not mean that I am actually doing so. But I believe that the desire to please you does in fact please you. And I hope I have that desire in all that I am doing. I hope that I will never do anything apart from that desire. And I know that if I do this you will lead me by the right road, though I may know nothing about it. Therefore I will trust you always though I may seem to be lost and in the shadow of death. I will not fear, for you are ever with me, and you will never leave me to face my perils alone.' (*Thoughts in Solitude*, p 83)